I set out to make Howdens feel like home: the sort of business our customers' fathers would have been proud to use.

We draw our inspiration from the thought that kitchens are the centre of our lives.. from the early morning cup of tea, our daily routine and the people we meet, to our return at the end of the day, and perhaps a mug of hot chocolate before bed. Whether fitting, using or simply enjoying the kitchen, Howdens is about the lives we lead, the encounters we have and the kitchens we all use.

Matthew Ingle

First published in the UK in 2010 by
Howden Joinery Ltd.
66 Chiltern Street
London
W1U 4JT
www.howdens.com

Printed and bound in the UK

ISBN 978-0-9563108-4-2

A Truly Local Business

An insight into the relationships that make Howden Joinery a part of local life all around Great Britain

Photographed on location in the UK

Series 005 Winter Edition

A Truly Local Business

Howden Joinery was founded in Yorkshire in 1995. Today, it is the UK's leading trade supplier of kitchens, employing over 5,000 people and supplying 240,000 small builders with around 4 million kitchen cabinets, 2 million doors and 400,000 complete kitchens – every year.

Despite its scale, Howdens remains a local business. It runs local customer accounts, not national ones; employees are engaged locally; profit-sharing is calculated locally, not centrally. Howdens operates successfully in over 460 different places, and in each one of them, the business is an integral part of local life.

At Howdens, our job is to try to solve problems for others – whether customers, colleagues or neighbours. They trust us not to let them down. We are committed to repaying their trust with good service, fair dealing and opportunities for all involved. Because real success, for Howdens, is about growing a great business that creates wealth, as well as profit.

We hope you enjoy this, the fifth in a series of books that celebrate the people who enrich the places where we live and work.

Supporting local treasures

Treasure & Son is a building contractors in Ludlow, Shropshire, which has been trading continuously for over 250 years. Treasure & Son has built a reputation for expertise in the renovation and conservation of old and historic buildings including the medieval castles at Ludlow, Warwick and Kenilworth.

Treasure & Son is a family business in the widest sense of the word: not only do they have a direct descendant of the founder on the current board of Directors, but also many employees are related to each another, and sons have followed fathers down the generations. This has helped to make a loyal, friendly and highly skilled workforce.

Gwynfor Benjamin has worked as a joiner all his life and has spent the last thirty seven years with Treasure & Son. He is also a regular cart driver in the 'Richards Castle Soap Box Derby' charity event in Ludlow. Gwynfor built his soap box in his garage from scrap, and has competed in the event for the last six years, raising over £6,000 in the process. The Howdens depot sponsor Gwynfor's soap box, and Gwynfor and Jerry Powell-Bevan, manager at the depot, are also retained firefighters at Ludlow Fire Station together.

Gwynfor Benjamin
Treasure & Son, Ludlow, Shropshire, December 2009

Negotiating dangerous waters

The Hamble lifeboat was formed in 1968 by local residents in response to the increasing number of casualties in Southampton Water and the Rivers Hamble, Itchen and Test. In the forty two years since it was founded, the lifeboat station has attended roughly 100 incidents a year, in all kinds of weather conditions.

Andrew Lynas has been a volunteer lifeboatman for the last two years. He has also been a sales representative at the local Howdens Joinery depot in Winchester since 2003.

Water based activities in the area are as popular as ever, so the next priority for the club is to replace its run-down lifeboat station. The current building has no hot water, heating, changing rooms, training facilities and is even too small to house the current lifeboats. Planning permission is in place and the Howdens depot has committed to help with the new build.

Andrew Lynas
Hamble, Hampshire, January 2010

Scaling the peaks

The Kinder Mountain Rescue Team, based in Hayfield in Derbyshire, is part of the Peak District Mountain Rescue Organisation. The team operates 365 days a year, seven days a week, twenty four hours a day, providing a mountain rescue service to walkers and climbers in the Peak District, as well as assisting the police with lowland search and rescue of vulnerable persons.

The rescue team is a registered charity and is self-funding. All fifty members of the mountain rescue team are also volunteers.

Chairman, Ken Blakeman, knows John Worthington at the Howdens Joinery depot in Stockport in Cheshire. John was happy to support the rescue team by donating a kitchen for the team headquarters.

Ken Blakeman, centre, and members of the
Kinder Mountain Rescue Team
Hayfield, High Peak, Derbyshire, November 2009

Trading blows

Russell Parsons has run his own loft conversion company for ten years, and has held an account at the Howdens Joinery depot in Christchurch in Dorset since 2004.

In September last year, Russell volunteered to take part in a 'white collar' boxing match in a charity night at Boscombe Opera House to raise money for local Children's Hospice, Julia's House.

Despite never having competed in boxing before, Russell trained five days a week, for seven weeks (losing two stone in the process) and made it through three rounds in front of two thousand cheering fans.

The night raised over 5000 pounds for the hospice, including donations from the Howdens depot.

Russell Parsons
Bulldog Sports Gym, Bournemouth, Dorset, December 2009

Providing a sanctuary

H.A.C.K. (Horse Aid, Care and Knowledge) is a sanctuary in Wrexham for distressed, neglected and cruelly treated horses, ponies and donkeys. The sanctuary provides food, shelter, grazing and veterinary care to the animals, where possible bringing them back into a normal working environment. In the eighteen years since the charity was originally registered, a great deal of experience, specialist training and dedication has helped well over 200 horses, ponies and donkeys.

The sanctuary is a registered charity, which relies on the generosity and good nature of its supporters, through a series of raffles, car boot sales, special appearances and adoptions. One of the volunteers knows Colin Roberts, the manager of the Howdens Joinery depot in Rhosddu in Wrexham. Colin was delighted to support H.A.C.K. by donating a kitchen for the sanctuary.

Jane Lloyd, Pamela Bluck and 'Westfield Red Fox'
H.A.C.K. Sanctuary, Wrexham, Clwyd, January 2010

Combining endurance and agility

As well as working behind the counter at the Howdens Joinery depot in Lymington for the last two and half years, Alex Gray is also a key member of the Southampton Crusaders Roller Hockey team. The Crusaders play their home games at the Applemore Health and Leisure Centre in Southampton and compete in the British Rink Hockey Association League.

In August 2009, Alex took part in the Goodwood Roller Marathon: a charity race around the historic Goodwood Motor Circuit in West Sussex. He entered the 26.62 'full' event completing eleven laps of the circuit in just over two hours. With the support of the depot and a number of trade customers, Alex raised over four hundred pounds for the NSPCC.

Alex Gray
Oaklands Leisure Centre, Southampton, Hampshire, December 2009

Leaping into the unknown

Adam Stoneham has worked at the Howdens Joinery depot in Worksop for four years. He started in the warehouse before moving to counter sales, and will shortly be going on the CAD training course. Adam's brother works in the depot warehouse, making it a true family affair.

Last year Adam challenged himself to do a parachute jump in order to raise money for the Weston Park Hospital Cancer Charity. The charity supports the work of Weston Park Hospital, which provides cancer treatment services for patients across Nottinghamshire and South Yorkshire, increasingly delivered in the community.

Note: Adam completed his 15,000 foot jump out of the 1979 Dornier G92 aircraft pictured here, and raised £500 for the charity.

Adam Stoneham
Hibaldstow Airfield, Brigg, Lincolnshire, December 2009

Establishing future relationships

Adam Willows and Dan Twells are both students on the 'Apprenticeship in Wood Occupations' Level 2 course at Derby College. The course is for 16-25 year olds interested in getting into the joinery and construction trade. It is made up of a number of units such as: Health and Safety, Workplace Efficiency, Access Equipment, First Fix, Second Fix, Carcassing, Power Tools and Employer Rights and Responsibilities.

Fran Jordan, manager at the Howdens Joinery depot in Derby, contacted the college last year in order to offer them discontinued products to assist with the course. The donated joinery doors, kitchen units, hardware and worktops are used to help the students refine their joinery skills and enable them to understand how the products are constructed.

It is hoped that this will become an ongoing mutually beneficial arrangement. The college gets products to help its students; the depot establishes early relationships with the future joiners of Derby.

Adam Willows and Dan Twells
Howdens Joinery depot, Derby, Derbyshire, January 2010

Supporting the referee

Zoe Pritchard lives and breathes football. She's been playing for thirteen years; she is Player/Manager of Madeley Sports FC Ladies First XI in Telford; she coaches football to Key Stage One and Three children in local schools in Shropshire; and she is a county standard referee.

Zoe's Aunt and Uncle, Andy Pritchard and Clare Walker, both work for the local Howdens Joinery depot in Telford. The depot has been happy to help Zoe with donations towards training equipment for the club.

Zoe Pritchard
Madeley Sports FC, Telford, Shropshire, September 2009

The Ministry of Food

The Ministry of Food is an initiative run by the City of Bradford Metropolitan District Council in association with chef Jamie Oliver. The Ministry is all about inspiring people to try home cooking and to live healthier lives. It takes its name from the World War II government department, appointed to help families make the most of wartime rations.

Jamie Oliver started the 'Ministry' movement in Rotherham, by teaching simple recipes and creating a centre to give non-cooks somewhere to learn basic kitchen skills. The centre in Bradford opened in November 2009, complete with kitchens and appliances from the Howdens Joinery depot in Bradford. Steve Keen (left) is the manager of the Howdens depot. Soraya Overend (centre) is the local Ministry of Food Project Manager. Russell Holroyd (right) was the Howdens designer on the project, planning out the kitchen, demonstration and teaching spaces.

The Council has been a direct customer of the Howdens depot for the last twelve years. As well as designing and supplying the kitchen and appliances, the depot donated kitchenware and trivets to the centre.

Steve Keen, Soraya Overend and Russell Holroyd
Ministry of Food, Bradford, West Yorkshire, January 2010

Engineering for the future

Antony Spring and Joe McKeegan are both serving Engineering Apprenticeships at St Helens College in Merseyside. Antony is in his second year of his Apprenticeship in Electrical/Electronic Engineering, and Joe is in his first year of his in Mechanical Engineering.

The college is proud of the reputation of its graduates, and a key part of both courses is time spent within industry, picking up real skills, as well as contributing to the output and culture of their employers.

Antony and Joe are the first St Helens College students selected to work as apprentices at the Howdens manufacturing site at Runcorn as part of their studies. They hope to finish their apprenticeships in 2012 and 2013 respectively, with Level Three National Certificates and some great experience.

Antony Spring and Joe McKeegan
Maintenance Workshop, Runcorn Manufacturing Facility, Cheshire,
January 2010

Pedalling hard

Tracey Olsson is a part time training administrator at the Howden manufacturing site, and has been working at Howden for over seventeen years.

In addition to her position at Howden, Tracey is also closely involved with the local community in Eastrington near Howden as a cycling proficiency trainer for the East Riding of Yorkshire Council.

Her cycling proficiency role involves teaching cycling skills to over 2,000 Year Five and Six school pupils, and pedestrian skills to over 3,300 Year Three and Four pupils each year. There has been some crossover between the roles: Tracey has completed a 'Health and Safety in the Workplace' course at Howdens, which assists with carrying out risk assessments in cycling proficiency training.

Tracey Olsson and trainee cyclists
Eastrington County Primary School, Howden, East Yorkshire,
January 2010

Out for the count

John Dickenson has been a member of the Bournemouth Amateur Boxing Club since 1961, and now acts as a boxing coach and Amateur Boxing Association judge at the club. The club itself has been going since 1948. It currently has over sixty members, and a number of volunteer trainers.

John is also a builder and has been fitting kitchens since he was fifteen years old. He has held an account with the Howdens Joinery depot in Poole, Dorset since 2000.

In October 2008 a fire literally reduced the club to its knees. The Howdens depot was happy to make a donation to the club to help get it back on its feet.

John Dickenson
Stokewood Leisure Centre, Bournemouth, Dorset, January 2010

Supporting a vital service

The Midlands Air Ambulance service has been saving lives for nearly twenty years and has flown more than 30,000 missions. The charity has an unrivalled reputation as a 'life saver', serving communities across six counties of the Midlands and Welsh border region.

It is generally accepted that the first hour after an accident is a crucial time for any patient. It is referred to as the 'Golden Hour'. If a patient reaches hospital during those first sixty minutes, the chances of survival are greatly increased. That's why the rapid response of the MAA's three Eurocopter aircraft is so vital in an emergency situation.

In terms of finances, it costs £5.6 million per year to run the three helicopters. However, according to NHS figures, it is believed that the cost of a person under the age of 35 who dies prematurely in an accident is over £1 million per patient. One such patient is saved every three weeks.

The MAA is run entirely based on charitable donations, as the service is not eligible for Government or Lottery funding. Terry Jones and the team at the Howdens Joinery depot in Merry Hill have been happy to help the service with charitable donations.

Andy Southall and Alison Blakeway
Merry Hill, West Midlands, January 2010

The Street Pastors

Street Pastors is an initiative set up by the Ascension Trust to help deal with today's challenge of anti-social behaviour with Christian advice at a local level. The Street Pastor's role is to engage with people on the streets and in night-time venues, by listening, supporting and offering practical help.

The scheme runs in over eighty areas in the UK and has been active in Lincoln for two years. Peter Gault and Donald Cornwell are members of the Lincoln team, who go out into Lincoln every Friday and Saturday night from 10.30 pm up until 5 am the next morning, offering advice, comfort, refreshment and a listening ear.

The Street Pastors are all volunteers and undergo twelve different training sessions on a variety of vital skills. Donald has been with Howdens for six years and has been a Senior Buyer at Howden for the last two years.

Peter Gault and Donald Cornwell
Lincoln Cathedral Quarter, Lincolnshire, December 2009

Performing nanorobotics

Year Seven students from Howden School and Technology College recently participated in the school's second cross-curricular 'nanorobotics' day. In the course of one day, teams of students were given the task of designing, building and presenting a 'nanorobot' capable of searching out and destroying cancer cells in the human body. The teams had to consider all aspects of their design, and present their solutions to the problems of power, propulsion, sensing, manipulation and removal.

The day was judged by Assistant Head, Simon Hadfield, along with Mark Livingston and Andy Locking from the Howdens Joinery manufacturing site at Howden. Howdens also provided the prizes for the winning teams.

The winning team from 7W
Howden School and Technology College, Howden, East Yorkshire,
January 2010

Running for a 'Great' cause

Stuart Taylor is the Assistant Manager at the Howdens Joinery depot in Fleetwood, Lancashire, and has been working for Howdens for nearly five years.

In September 2009, Stuart was part of a group of fifteen members of staff from Howdens' Northern region who took part in the Great North Run. Following three months' training, he completed the 13.1 mile course, one of the biggest and most popular running events in the world, and raised over five hundred pounds towards a new minibus for the charity. Stuart was supported by his depot, account holders, friends and family.

Stuart Taylor
Fleetwood, Lancashire, September 2009

Applying skills to good causes

Peter Speight is an engineering manager at the Howden Manufacturing site in East Yorkshire. He has been with the company for nearly three years after a long career in the Army. In his role he is also qualified as a Chartered Institute of Environmental Health trainer.

In his spare time, Peter devotes a significant amount of time to the New Life Church in Scunthorpe, and also to the Lighthouse: a homeless shelter also in Scunthorpe.

Peter has been a member of the New Life church since 2000. In that time he has been able to apply his skills to project manage, design and fit a new foyer for the church.

He also volunteers for the Lighthouse. The homeless shelter is in the premises of a thirteen bedroom former B&B in Scunthorpe. In addition to providing short to medium term housing, the centre offers training and coaching in many areas ranging from debt advice and financial literacy, to parentcraft and marriage skills. As well as volunteering, Peter has again been able to help with improvements to the building.

Peter Speight
New Life Church, Scunthorpe, Lincolnshire, January 2010

Supporting community spirit

Concerned about the rise in anti-social behaviour in East Worthing, local residents Mick and Chriss Smith decided to engage with local teenagers. Mick started off in 2002 by mending their bikes in his own garage at home. The garage quickly evolved into a focal point for the area, and now Mick and Chriss run a community house, attended by more than 6,000 children and their families every year. They run activities such as: cookery with children, baking for coffee mornings, taking children on trips, after-school clubs, as well as valuable IT facilities where children can do their homework. The centre itself was donated by local housing association, Worthing Homes, in partnership with children's charity, Spurgeons.

Through account holders, Luda Interiors, the local Howdens Joinery depot in Worthing supply all the kitchens for Worthing Homes. Mick and Chriss asked the Howdens depot for an oven and hob for the centre's kitchen. The depot was delighted to donate a complete kitchen including worktops and cupboards for the centre, which was also fitted for free by Luda.

Chriss and Mick Smith
East Worthing, West Sussex, December 2009

Working in partnership

Howdens Joinery has a close relationship on a national and local level with Leonard Cheshire Disability. The charity aims to change attitudes to disability and to serve disabled people around the world. In the UK, the main activity is the provision of care homes, supported living, domiciliary support, day services, resource centres, rehabilitation, respite care, personal support and training and assistance for those looking for work.

Working with Bill Everett at Howdens, local depots throughout the UK have been working with Leonard Cheshire Disability centres to help them design, supply and install truly inclusive kitchen facilities. Increasing involvement has enabled Howdens to develop kitchen products, which offer people of all abilities the same level of choice.

The Beechwood Cheshire Home has been serving the local community in Huddersfield for nearly fifty years. It offers twenty six rooms for residents as well as a small day care service. Thanks to the arrangement with Howdens, the home has been fitted with a new kitchen for the residents and day residents to use for preparing their own meals and drinks. This is a key part of enabling them to retain their independence. The kitchen is also used for teaching basic cooking skills to those residents, who are moving back out into the community.

Liz Cwalina and Tim Owen
Beechwood Cheshire Home, Huddersfield, West Yorkshire, January 2010

Supporting local schools and the joiners of the future

Tim Vernon is a technology teacher and the Head of Year Nine at Bramhall High School in Cheshire. The school is a mixed comprehensive with just under 1,400 students. Its Design and Technology department was recently recognised nationally as a 'Centre of Excellence' and was invited to London to deliver a presentation on how to achieve outstanding results.

Following the success of his relationship with Stockport College (Truly Local Summer 2009 edition), John Worthington, manager of the Howdens Joinery depot in Stockport, has established a similar arrangement with Bramhall High School. Year Seven students receive discontinued joinery products from Howdens to help them with their 'Resistant Materials' module. The depot also supplies Howdens branded tools and tool bags for the school.

Tim Vernon
Bramhall High School, Bramhall, Cheshire, January 2010

Rewarding experiences

During each sales period every Howdens depot manager enjoys a meal, traditionally a curry, with the company's Sales Director and Chief Executive. The evenings are a feature of the business, offering a valuable chance to share views and experiences from each of the 462 local marketplaces Howdens operates in, as well as offering support to local restaurants throughout the country.

This year Howdens decided to challenge the regions to find the best local Indian restaurant with judging taking place across the country during September. In 2009 the 'India Gate' restaurant in Dunblane, Perthshire won the prize for themselves and the Scottish region.

Khimlal Panday and Aishwarya Bahadur Khadka
India Gate Restaurant, Dunblane, Perthshire January 2010

Glossary

Account holders – each year, Howdens Joinery supplies over 240,000 registered account holders, mostly small builders.

British Rink Hockey Association League – formed in 1985, the league has grown from three senior teams to eighteen teams of various age groups.

Cycling Proficiency - a test given by the Royal Society for the Prevention of Accidents (RoSPA) which serves as a minimum recommended standard for cycling on British roads.

Depot - Howdens Joinery has 462 depots across the country, where local staff serve local tradespeople

Goodwood Motor Circuit - situated on the estate of Goodwood house, the circuit began life as the perimeter track of RAF Westhampnett airfield which was constructed during World War II as a relief airfield for RAF Tangmere.

Great North Run - the world's second most popular half marathon road running event. Devised by former Olympic 10,000 m bronze medallist Brendan Foster after running in the Round the Bays Race in New Zealand in 1979.

Glossary

Kinder Scout - a moorland plateau (and mountain) in the Dark Peak of the Derbyshire Peak District in England. At 2,087 feet (636 m) above sea level, it is the highest point in the Peak District and Derbyshire.

The Ministry of Food (1939-1954) - British government ministerial body separated from that of the Minister of Agriculture between 1939 and 1954. A major task of the office was to oversee rationing in the United Kingdom arising out of World War II.

Nanorobotics – the technology of creating machines or robots at or close to the microscopic scale of a nanometer.

White Collar Boxing - a growing sport, for company executives who also enjoy the training, camaraderie and excitement of amateur boxing.

This book is printed on FSC certified paper

ere the brothers were
ten to be found after
long days work.

The Crown

The Orchard

Post Office

HOWDENS